Monster P␣␣␣␣␣␣␣␣␣
1st edition 2014

© Mike Amos-Simpson

All rights reserved, no part of this book may be reproduced in any format without prior permission.

Designed and typeset by YoMo Creative

The associated resources with this story may be freely reproduced for use within school classrooms and for educational activities providing they have been purchased by the school or educational provider responsible for using them.

www.learningpower.co.uk

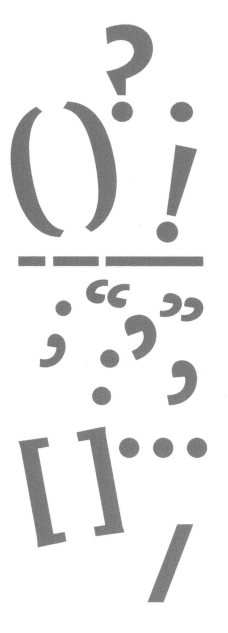

Contents

YoMo

LEARNING POWER

Mike Amos-Simpson is a founder member of the literacy charity, STORIES4CHANGE. He helps school children exchange illustrated stories between Malawi and the UK that are created by the children and then professionally finished and published.

Previously Mike established the national Young Movers Programme that supported young people living in areas of deprivation to develop their personal skills through project based learning.

He has provided training based on practical activities to support children and young people's personal development for over a decade; working with teachers, youth workers and volunteers across the UK, Ireland, Tanzania and Malawi.

YoMo Learning Power consists of activity based resources to help students think creatively and develop awareness of their personal skills

Resources are designed to support teachers to help children and young people develop their personal learning skills and abilities.

Often referred to as 'soft skills', personal skills are the 'X-factor' of learning and are key to personal character.

Introduction

This is not a book about the usage of punctuation, plenty of those monsters already exist. Instead this book is about *punctuation marks*. It aims to stimulate interest about how punctuation has varied and developed with the ultimate aim of stimulating curiosity and understanding in something that bewilders many of us for most of our lives.

The Punctuation Monsters each have an individual chapter including a collection of history and facts related to the dots and squiggles we know today as punctuation marks.

Before you get to the monsters there is a timeline to demonstrate how written English and punctuation has developed. The events included are not necessarily the most significant aspects of history, but they demonstrate how written English has not simply evolved but has instead hopped, jumped and skipped into the modern day format, sometimes by nothing more than a printer's whim.

The book ends with details of accompanying resources and activity ideas designed to help students develop their interest through exploration and experimentation with the shapes and functions of punctuation marks. They can colour in monsters and create their own. They can make up stories and think about personalities and behaviours of different punctuation monsters. And they can take on the challenge of creating new punctuation marks; they won't be the first to do so?

What is the **POINT?**

Pointing is an old term for punctuating, making 'pointless punctuation' an oxymoron!

In the 14th century the word point meant anything that looked like a dot and had been taken from Old French meaning the 'smallest amount'.

Common definitions included:

- pricking, stabbing, jabbing, marking
- the marking of points when writing became known as pointing

The term punctuation came into use from the 17th century and is taken from 'punctus' in Latin (meaning 'prick').

Punctilious

Punctilious: great attention to detail or correct behaviour. Probably taken from the Italian 'puntiglioso' originally referring to a 'fine point'.

Perhaps there never existed on any subject, among men of learning, a greater difference of opinion than on the true mode of punctuation. Some sprinkle title page with commas almost as promiscuously as if from a pepper-box ; some make the pause of a semicolon where the sense will only bear a comma ; some contending for what is termed stiff pointing, and others for altogether the reverse.

A Manual of Typography, 1871 **5**

The
24th September

is National Punctuation Day
in the United States.

Apostrophe

Single Quote

Comma

Punctate: studded with dots or tiny holes (Biology)

Punctiform: resembling a small dot

Punctilio: a fine or pretty point of conduct or procedure

Punctual: Relating to an action at a particular point in time

Punctuate: insert punctuation marks in text

Punctum: a point or small area (anatomy)

Puncture: a small hole

Punk Rocker: person that enjoys dotty music and fashion

'SHARE'
Students Punctuation Monsters...

by emailing images of them to:
comma@monsterpunctuation.co.uk

Writing is an expressive medium. Creative expression is difficult with rules, particularly rules that often make little sense and that are openly contradicted. It is important that we seek not to limit children with the 'rules' of writing, but instead equip them with the tools to write appropriately and effectively and with the confidence to experiment.

As children are taught that a semicolon is something stuck between independent clauses connected by conjunctive adverbs or transitional phrases, they're also exchanging text messages with their friends — OMG!?!

Modern forms of written communication have already had their impact on language. We write and read in more ways than at any point in history. For the most part we can choose exactly how we prefer to go about writing because there is not, and never has been, any definitive body for the English language. There are no rules — only tools.

While this allows for considerable creativity, it also assumes an element of responsibility to ensure we use appropriate forms of expressing ourselves in writing. If not we risk being misunderstood and it is to this aim that punctuation serves — to help us express ourselves as we intend.

Use the Punctuation Monsters to stimulate students interest and understanding of punctuation, and help them prepare to tackle the biggest monstrosity of all... the Red Inker.

Have fun :-)

Mike Amos-Simpson

Writing & Punctuation
Timeline

3,200 BCE

First Known Writing System

Modern humans have walked the earth for around 200,000 years. They started writing just 5,000 years ago.

The earliest known writing system was in Mesopotamia (modern day Iraq). People there used clay tablets to record figures for agriculture and commerce and this eventually evolved into the Sumerian Writing System from around 3,200BCE

Writing systems emerged at a similar time in Egypt and were followed by independent systems later in China (1,200BCE) and Mesoamerica (900BCE).

Early writing methods used pictograms — simple pictures of what was being written about.

Circles are difficult to draw in clay and so the pictures were often simplified to use straight lines. In addition to representing visual images, symbols were also used to describe the phonetic sound of a word by using images that sounded like the word.

Papyrus

The Egyptians developed their writing system to use rolls of paper made with papyrus plants. This was written on by using sharpened reeds dipped in ink and allowed for a more flexible and descriptive form of writing.

Evolution of the Sumerian Writing System
Early drawings were drawn from top-down. Later people began to write from left-to-right and the images were rotated. Over time the images developed into more abstract symbols.

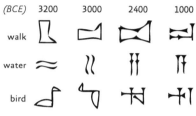

Thoth

2,560 BCE

Egyptian scribes studied for years and could achieve prestige and power in society.

Writing was said to have been a gift from the Egyptian God Thoth and Egyptian hieroglyphs were known as the 'writing of the Gods'.

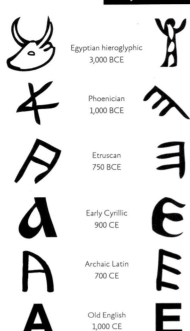

1,050 BCE

Egyptian hieroglyphic
3,000 BCE

Phoenician
1,000 BCE

Etruscan
750 BCE

Early Cyrillic
900 CE

Archaic Latin
700 CE

Old English
1,000 CE

English was written with Anglo-Saxon runes from about the 5th century. The Latin alphabet used by Christian missionaries replaced the runes about 200 years later although both the runic and Latin alphabets were in use until the 10th century.

In the year 1011 a monk recorded the English alphabet with 24 Latin letters and five additional letters. The Latin letters included the ampersand (&) which was considered as a latter of the alphabet until very recently. It would be over 500 years before J and U appeared in the alphabet (see page 20).

ABCDE
FGHIK
LMNOP
QRSTV
XYZ&⁊
ƿ Þ Ð Æ

840 BCE

300 BCE

Phoenician Alphabet

Nearly all writing systems started initially as pictograms before evolving into symbols that are simpler and quicker to use. Mastering early writing systems required memorising hundreds of symbols making them difficult and time-consuming to learn.

The development of alphabets simplified writing. Alphabets use combinations of a set number of symbols to describe words and are much simpler to learn.

The Phoenician alphabet is the first known alphabet and quickly became used and adapted throughout the Mediterranean.

Prior to the alphabet, writing had required considerable education and written communications were used to restrict information to the upper classes. The new simpler method of writing challenged this divide.

The Greek alphabet is descended from Phoenician.

Oldest Punctuation

The earliest example of punctuation is on the Mesha Stele – an inscribed stone written in the Moabite language and using dots and lines to punctuate.

Latin Alphabet

The alphabet from which our modern writing descends appeared around 300BCE. The Latin alphabet spread with the Roman Empire. The word 'alphabet' is taken from the Greek from which it descends: 'Alpha' 'Beta'.

Early.Punctuation·System˙

A Greek scholar, Aristophones of Byzantium, proposed a system of punctuation using dots at different heights. The system wasn't widely used at the time. (see page 30)

·INTERPUNCT·

75 BCE

The Romans sometimes used dots (or triangles) known as interpuncts to separate words. The practice fell out of use from about 200CE after which most writing used the Greek system of 'scriptio continua' (writing without spaces or dividers).

Early Punctuation Guide

Archbishop Isidore of Seville wrote a detailed guide to punctuation in his encyclopedia 'Etymologiae'

In addition to the same system of dots proposed by Aristophones of Byzantium 800 years earlier, Isidore describes an accent known as an 'Astrophus' that is placed at the top of a letter to indicate the final vowel in a word is lacking. He also describes various 'critical signs' used to annotate writing.

SpacesBetweenWords

Irish monks began the practice of using 'white space' to separate written words. The practise was gradually adopted across Europe.

When letters are grouped into words and framed by white space, the words are simpler to read, making the process of reading much quicker.

200 BCE

Distinctio (periodos)

Media distinctio (komma)

Sub distinctio (colon)

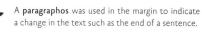

ΔΠCΦΞΠT GRΞΞK

Diples were used in margins to draw attention to certain text.

Before the use of spaces a **hypodiastole** separated words that might otherwise be confused.

A **paragraphos** was used in the margin to indicate a change in the text such as the end of a sentence.

Current Era

600 CE

Among the signs described by Isidore, the 'Cryphia' (shown to the right) signified a difficult or obscure question that could not be resolved.

600 BCE

EARLYWRITINGWASMOSTLYUSEDFOR
READINGALOUDANDWASMEMORISED
WITHTHEWRITINGUSEDTOREMEMBER
THEWORDSPUNCTUATIONANDSPACES
BETWEENWORDSWERENOTNEEDED
AMODERNFORMOFSCRIPTIOCONTINUA
ISUSEDFORSOMEWEBSITEADDRESSES

Early texts like bibles were designed to be read aloud and early punctuation assisted with reading aloud.

700 CE

Anglo-Saxon Scribes Tinker

Possibly encouraged by their Irish counterparts, Anglo-Saxon scribes started adding marks to texts to help their countrymen better understand texts in the foreign language of Latin.

These early marks don't much relate to modern punctuation as without an agreed system they varied considerably in use and looks. As their purpose was to assist text to be read aloud they also differed in function from modern punctuation.

One innovation was the use of diples to indicate quoted text. Initially diples appeared only in the margins and again there were variations in use and appearance. By the end of the 8th century the diple as a quotation mark disappeared and it would be over half a millennium before modern quotation marks emerged.

The beautifully ornamental 'hedera' (Latin for ivy) was used in very early Greek and Roman texts to divide sections of text. By the middle ages it was more often used as an ornament or to distinguish text from commentary. In the US the hedera is known as the 'floral heart'.

The diple is very old and was used in Ancient Greek texts as a symbol to draw attention to particular text.

A double-diple known as a 'guillemet' is used by the French as a modern quotation mark. They are named after a 16th century printer called Guillaume Le Bé.

800 CE

Consistent Writing Style

Charlemagne, crowned Emperor of Europe in 800CE was said to have hidden wax tablets under his pillow to practice writing letters. Despite his efforts he was barely literate but he valued literacy highly.

He enlisted a scholar from England — Alcuin of York, to run his 'scriptorium'. Alcuin helped develop a consistent writing style known as the Carolingian Minuscule that enabled texts to be more easily understood across the different regions of Charlemagne's empire and beyond.

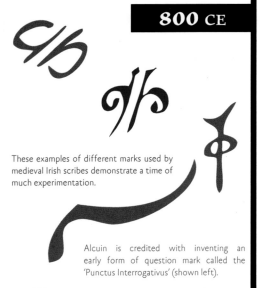

These examples of different marks used by medieval Irish scribes demonstrate a time of much experimentation.

Alcuin is credited with inventing an early form of question mark called the 'Punctus Interrogativus' (shown left).

Carolingian Minuscule

Alfred the Great

Alfred became the King of Wessex in 871 and is regarded as the first 'king of the Anglo-Saxons'.

He used Christianity to further his ambitions to unify England while fending off the threat of the Danes. Like Charlemagne, Alfred valued literacy and he invested in an education system. He advocated that primary education be taught in English and organised for books to be translated into English to support it.

> " *Therefore I think it better... that we also translate certain books, which is most needful for all men to know, into the language that we can all understand...[and] that all young people who are now freemen in England... should devote themselves to study... until the time that they know how to read written English well.* "
>
> Alfred the Great, King of Wessex

Though referred to as 'English', Britain was a place of many variations in language. The most widely spoken language in Wessex was West Saxon while Northern England was ruled by the Old Norse tongue of the Danes. By capturing the 'common language' in writing Alfred helped establish what we refer to today as Old English but England would continue to be multilingual for many years.

Alfred died in 899 but the House of Wessex finally unified England in 927. Under a hundred years later England fell to Danish rule. As the Vikings and Anglo-Saxons continued their wrestle for power, the French moved in...

The Anglo-Saxon Chronicle originates from Alfred's reign and details the history of England from Roman times to beyond the Norman Conquest. The section below from the Peterborough Chronicle in the 12th century, explains that Britain is 800 miles long by 200 miles wide and has five nations: English, British (Welsh & Scotch), Pictish and Romans.

The Peterborough Chronicle is the most recent of the chronicles and is written in both Old English and Middle English.

11

1000 CE

-HYPHEN-

1066 CE

Almost a third of English words originate from French. While the English peasants were farming, the French nobility enjoyed eating the meat:

English *(Old English)*	(English) French *(Old French)*
cow *(cu)*	(beef) **bœuf** *(buef)*
sheep *(sceap)*	(mutton) **mouton** *(moton)*
swine *(swin)*	(pork) **porc** *(porc)*
calf *(cealf)*	(veal) **veau** *(veel)*
deer *(deor*)*	(venison) **venison** *(venesoun)*

*deor meant 'wild animal'

1100 CE

The 'Punctus Elevatus' was used between the 12th and 15th centuries before being replaced by the semicolon.

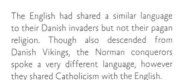

1300 CE

The English had shared a similar language to their Danish invaders but not their pagan religion. Though also descended from Danish Vikings, the Norman conquerors spoke a very different language, however they shared Catholicism with the English.

After 1066 the King of England also ruled Normandy, but in 1337 King Edward III felt he should be the king of France too.

The 'Hundred Years War' eventually led to the English nobility losing their power in France and Normandy but it also gave rise to English nationalism and the English language survived a second invasion.

The-Hyphen-Dashes-in

An early version of the hyphen was - used during the 11th century to - indicate that words continued on - the next line.

Language of the Peasants

After William the Bastard became William the Conqueror, he removed power and land from Anglo-Saxons and gifted them to his Norman friends. Old English became the language of the peasants and the defeated.

A little over a hundred years after the Norman conquest a university was established in Oxford, followed shortly by another in Cambridge. Literacy in England increased, but not English literacy as the commoners language became a largely unwritten language. While English was spoken by the native population, Latin was the language of writing and the educated and French was the language of nobility and governance.

Eventually the Norman nobility came to regard themselves as English to the extent that from 1337 the Anglo-Normans embarked on fighting the French for the next 116 years.

During this period French became the language of the enemy and Old English (by now developed into 'Middle English') rose in prominence.

The Black Death (1348-9) impacted language too — killing off between a third and half the English population including a disproportionate amount of the Latin speaking clergy.

The Father of English Literacy

Chaucer was born shortly before the Black Death devastated England. He lived his life through the Hundred Years War, working mostly as a civil servant. He was captured by the French in 1360 but freed after the payment of a ransom (paid in part by King Edward III).

Chaucer wrote his famous Canterbury Tales in the late 14th century and he wrote it in English. French and Latin were well established written languages, but the spoken language of English still varied greatly between regions. Chaucer wrote of his concern:

❝ *For ther is so gret diversite in Englissh and in writyng of oure tonge* ❞

Today he is credited as the first person to write down about two thousand English words and has been admired not only as a historical figure but also during his lifetime was referred to by a contemporary as "the firste fyndere of our fair langage".

Guilty Monsieur

The 'Pleading in English' Act of 1362 stipulated that English was to be the spoken language of the court (previously it had been French). Latin remained the written language.

Colon:

Colons popped into writing during the late 14th century.

1343 CE

Chaucer captured many English words in writing for the first time, many of which are still in use today:

bum quack fart poop þ

English had now developed into Middle English which is more understandable to us than the Old English used during Anglo-Saxon times. In The Summoners Tale Chaucer tells the story of Thomas who gifted to a friar a fart louder than a horse:

> Amydde his hand he leet the frere a fart;
> Ther nys no capul, drawynge in a cart,
> That myghte have lete a fart of swich a soun.

> Amid his hand he let the friar a fart;
> There is no horse, pulling a cart,
> That could have let a fart of such a sound.

scyld scefing mæþum meo eopl syððan cepef

Beowulf ◇

Beowulf is the oldest surviving poem written in Old English. The poem was written by an Anglo-Saxon between the 8th & 11th centuries and tells the adventures of a Scandinavian hero who became a King. The Anglo-Saxons were descended from Scandinavian and Northern Germanic people.

1362 CE

The Pleading in English Act was written in French!

1390 CE

Chinese is the oldest continually used writing system in the world.

An educated person would need to memorise about 4,000 characters to be literate in Chinese which does not use an alphabet.

Developments like Simplified Chinese (used to the right) aim to improve Chinese literacy and help with the practical application of the language.

Gutenberg's main innovation was a hand mould that allowed letters to be quickly cast for the purpose of setting type ready for print. His 'punch' enabled about 4,000 letters to be cast a day.

Early printers attempted to replicate the hand written styles of copyists, but new typefaces soon led to the distinct modern style of print that we are familiar with today.

The Father of Modern Printing

The Chinese were making paper in 105CE but kept their methods secret until it was revealed 650 years later after some Arabs beat them in a battle. Shortly after, paper manufacturing began in Iraq — the same part of the world that people had started writing on clay tablets 4,000 years earlier.

Paper-making spread along the Silk Road and into Europe by the 11th century. A paper mill opened in Mainz, Germany in 1320 and a century later Johannes Gutenberg revealed his 'movable type' printing press.

As ever the Chinese had already started printing, but in China the process was slow and complex due to the vast amount of characters in the Chinese writing system. European writing with its limited alphabet was better suited to mechanised printing.

Gutenberg's printing press along with the availability of paper effectively invented the modern book and would subsequently lead to modern grammar and punctuation, typography and a rapid acceleration of literacy.

None of this benefited Gutenberg who lived a life in debt and resided in a city in the midst of a religious feud, a feud that ultimately led to Gutenberg and his family being exiled from his home city of Mainz until just a few years before his death in 1468.

The unrest in Mainz caused the print industry to relocate too, primarily to Italy.

The Father of English Printing

William Caxton was a successful businessman born in England but living in Bruges. He was a book collector and wrote for pleasure.

In 1471 at age 50, he completed a three year undertaking of the translation of the French book 'Recuyell of the Historyes of Troye' for the Duchess of Burgundy. She liked it so much she requested more copies. Caxton wrote each copy by hand until in 1473 he presented a copy in which he wrote:

> ❝ *Therfore I haue practysed & lerned at my grete charge and dispense to ordeyne this said book in prynte after the maner & forme as ye may here see /and is not wreton with penne and ynke as other bokes* ❞

Caxton had practised and learned to 'prynte' (print).

Caxton subsequently established the first printing press in England in 1476 and began printing books created in England and printed in English. One of the first books he printed was Chaucer's Canterbury Tales.

There is only limited punctuation in Caxton's works and he is considered to be more a businessman than an artist. However he was prolific and despite starting late in life, he successfully printed 100 titles.

After his death Caxton's print house was taken over by Wynkyn de Worde who relocated the business to become the first printer in Fleet Street.

1476 CE

A 'printers mark' or 'device' was a symbol used as a kind of trademark. Caxton's mark shows the initials 'WC' and the numbers '47'. The significance of the numbers isn't known but may refer to the year Caxton gained the Freedom of the Mercers' Company (1447) after years of serving an apprenticeship.

mp penne is worn

Caxton wrote of his hand written books *'My pen is worn, mine hand heavy, my eye even dimmed'*

In 1998 a copy of Caxton's first edition Canterbury Tales sold for £4.6 million!

Caxton used little punctuation except for the 'solidus' (the slash) which was commonly used as a comma at the time.

Caxton first used a Batarda typeface

Bastarda (bâtarde/bastard) scripts were used by scribes in France and Germany to copy texts of minor importance. Gutenberg produced the earliest printed bastarda.

eggys or egges (eggs)

Caxton faced new challenges that would eventually shape the English language. One of these was choosing how to print English that could be understandable to people that spoke the language differently across the country. The choices he made inevitably influenced how English words would be subsequently written by others.

The choices printers made were not always for the benefit of comprehension. Sometimes an extra 's' or 'es' would be added to words simply to help them fit better on the line!

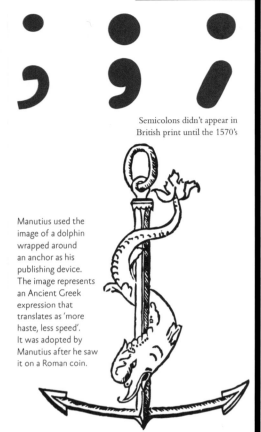

Semicolons didn't appear in British print until the 1570's

Manutius used the image of a dolphin wrapped around an anchor as his publishing device. The image represents an Ancient Greek expression that translates as 'more haste, less speed'. It was adopted by Manutius after he saw it on a Roman coin.

The punchcutter, Francesco Griffo, who designed the elegant typefaces used by Manutius (including italic), disappeared from history after being accused of murdering his son-in-law.

The slash had been in common use as a comma. Manutius gave it a curve and moved it lower to create the modern comma.

First Printed Semicolon;

The earliest known printed semicolon appears in 'De Aetna' printed by the Italian, Aldus Manutius in 1495.

> Quia noueram mores hominum ;tum
> etiam pertentare te prorfus uolui ,q̃ recte
> ifta fentires. Sed omittamus haec iam tan
> dem fili ; atq; ad eam partem fermonis,

Venice was considered the European capital of printing and Manutius considered its leading printer.

The Aldine Press founded by Manutius printed 'pocket sized' books from 1501. The smaller books were made possible due to the invention of a smaller condensed typeface known at the time as 'Aldine Type' and better known today as *italic*.

The new smaller books were portable, less expensive and printed in greater quantities. They were beautifully presented and assiduously designed and very popular.

Despite efforts to prevent others copying his work, Manutius's methods were widely copied and became the model for the modern book.

His usage of punctuation marks were also replicated and Manutius is credited with introducing the modern semicolon and comma and 'normalising' modern punctuation.

While the early printers introduced many of the modern punctuation marks, it would take considerably longer before people agreed on how to use them; arguably they never would...

Chancery English

Normandy born Richard Pynson was appointed as the King's Printer in 1506.

His use of 'Chancery English', which was largely based on the London and East Midlands dialects, significantly influenced the standardisation of the written form of Early Modern English.

Architect of the English Language

Reading an English translation of the Bible was illegal. Translating the Bible into English was *really* illegal!! But William Tyndale was determined to do it anyway and so he moved to Europe and alternated writing with running away from a lot of very angry people.

His translations were printed in 1526 and then banned in England and copies were publicly burned. Tyndale continued to be hunted by King Henry VIII and the Pope and eventually was betrayed to the Court of The Holy Roman Emperor.

Tyndale was burned at the stake in 1536 uttering the final plea: *"Lord, open the king of England's eyes"*. Unknown to him was that Henry had already commissioned a new bible to be used in his newly created Church of England.

Published three years after Tyndale's execution, much of The Great Bible was copied from the Tyndale Bible. Tyndale's work and the language he used was to be heard in churches throughout the country.

1506 CE

The Court of the Chancery dealt with legal issues.

Scriveners wrote letters and legal documents, often on behalf of people that could not read or write themselves.

Consistent meaning and understanding is important for legal matters and so the use of particular words and their meaning would have been very important for scriveners of the Chancery.

1526 CE

eate drinke and be mery

he bowed him selfe and fell flatt on his face

to heale the broken harted

Tyndale was highly educated and fluent in many languages. The bibles based on his work meant that his style of writing influenced many others and was significant in the development to 'Early Modern English'. Many phrases are attributed to him including:

eat drink and be merry	the powers that be
the salt of the earth	under the sun
broken-hearted	the land of the living
fall flat on his face	pour out one's heart
signs of the times	go the extra mile
skin of your teeth	fight the good fight

ye are ye salt of the erthe

The powers that be are ordeyned of God.

The King James Bible was first published in 1611.

As the British Empire spread across the world, the King James Bible became the most widely used Bible in the English speaking world. Today it is thought to be the best selling book of all time and the most quoted book in the English language.

More than 80% of the King James Bible is based on William Tyndale's Bible.

The Captain of the Golden Hind expressed concern about the sea worthiness of Sir Humphrey Gilbert's ship, HMS Squirrel, on the return journey from America but Gilbert refused the invitation to switch ships.

Gilbert was said to have been reading Sir Thomas More's book 'Utopia' which includes the words:

"He that hathe no grave is covered with the skye: and, the way to heaven out of all places is of like length and distance."

The crew of the Golden Hind reported hearing Gilbert call repeatedly from his ship: *"We are as near to Heaven by sea as by land!"* while pointing to the sky.

The HMS Squirrel sank in the middle of the night on the 9th September. Gilbert and all aboard would never be found.

Extract of illustration from the first edition of Utopia published in 1516

k:L.l.ľ:M.m.ḿ:N.n.ń: ŕ:S.ſ.s.ʒ:ꟸ.ſh.ꟶ:T.t:Ⱨ.

Prior to publishing English Grammar, Bullokar had proposed a new 40 letter phonetic alphabet for the English language.

On the title page of the first edition of Table Alphabeticall, 'words' is spelled in two different ways!

A Table Alphabeticall, con-
teyning and teaching the true
writing, and vnderstanding of hard
vsuall English wordes, borrowed from
the Hebrew, Greeke, Latine,
or French. &c.

With the interpretation thereof by
plaine English words, gathered for the benefit &
helpe of Ladies, Gentlewomen, or any other
vnskilfull persons.

Legere, et non intelligere, neglegere est.
As good not read, as not to vnderstand.

AT LONDON,
Printed by I. R. for Edmund Wea-
uer, & are to be sold at his shop at the great
North doore of Paules Church.
1604.

New Empire: New Grammar

In September 1580, Francis Drake sailed the Golden Hind into Plymouth having circumnavigated the globe (and raided Spanish ships along the way).

Three years later Sir Humphrey Gilbert took *'possession of NEW FOUND LAND in the name of his sovereign Queen Elizabeth [and] thereby founded Britain's overseas empire'.*

As the first British Empire expanded, so did the English language and interest in how the language should be structured and understood grew too.

The first published English grammar was created by the printer, William Bullokar in 1586. This was followed eight years later by the first English dictionary — Table Alphabeticall created by a schoolteacher, Robert Cawdrey who wrote of his concern about people...

" *...forgetting altogether their mothers language, so that if some of their mothers were alive, they were not able to tell or vnderstand what they say... far journied gentlemen* [collect words on their travels and] *pouder their talke with over-sea language.* **"**

Neither of these early 'grammarians' had much impact but they represent the beginning of a concern between those intent on capturing and preserving a language as it inevitably changes and evolves beyond their control.

Other people had their own ideas...

The Apostrophe Arrive's

In Love's Labor's Lost, William Shakespeare included the line:

"You finde not the apostraphas, and so misse the accent."

In doing so he delighted English grammarians who could enjoy debating correct use of the apostrophe for the next few hundred years.

Although the apostrophe had been in use long before Shakespeare's time, the apostrophes in the title of Love's Labor's Lost didn't actually appear until 50 years after his death!

Nonetheless Shakespeare has been credited with inventing the word 'apostrophe' and the role of punctuation in his plays remains the subject of hot debate.

No matter what Shakespeare contributed to the English language, he can't be credited for any form of punctuation because although widely considered the greatest ever English writer... there are no known examples of his actual writing.

While Shakespeare did not write for print but instead wrote for the benefit of people 'lending their ears', his work nonetheless contributed to an increased interest (and market)in fictional writing.

Away, you scullion, you rampallion, you fustilarian! I'll tickle your catastrophe.

King Henry IV Shakespeare

how well he's read to reason against reading

Shakespeare was a playwright for an acting company famous for their plays performed at the Globe theatre — the King's Men.

Shakespeare's name was attractive enough for printers to create 'pirate' versions of his work. The first printed version of Romeo and Juliet in 1597 was such a work.

Most of what is considered as Shakespeare's 'writing' was actually written on his behalf by fellow actors who compiled the 36 plays known as the First Folio after his death.

Introducing the works they had written on Shakespeare's behalf they wrote:

"[we wish he] had liv'd to have set forth and overseen his owne writings"

while noting that:

"[people had previously been] abus'd with diverse stoln and surreptitious copies... by the frauds and stealthes of injurious imposters..."

Nonetheless they chose to use a printer famous for having previously printed pirate versions of Shakespeare's work (known as the False Folio).

There are no known manuscripts, notes or letters written by William Shakespeare. All of his written works were compiled by others and have subsequently been altered and edited by printers and editors over generations.

The 'apostrophus' looked like a backward 'C' and was used in the Ancient Roman number system. It had been used as a punctuation mark as early as 1501 by Aldus Manutius and appeared in print in England in 1559 in William Cunningham's 'Cosmographical Glasse'.

The term 'apostrophe' was reference to a speaker breaking away from speaking to an audience to speak instead to a third party.

The apostrophas/apostrophus can be seen across texts written in the 16th century to indicate the omission of letters, for example lov'd for loved.

It didn't become the modern apostrophe or mean anything to do with possession until the 18th century.

1621 CE

Though he would never have described himself as such, Ben Jonson was a playwright *(he would have considered himself a poet)*.

Although it was written at a time of much experimentation, the punctuation described in Jonson's book remains familiar today.

Jonson referenced the 'alphabet with its 'twenty and four letters' (J and I were absent). J was a variation of 'I' and had appeared shortly before English Grammar was published. 'U' was considered as a form of 'V' and was never used at the beginning of a word *(only in the middle and ends)*. A capital U was therefore considered unnecessary by printers.

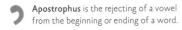 **Apostrophus** is the rejecting of a vowel from the beginning or ending of a word.

 A **subdistinction**… when the word serveth indifferently, both to parts of the sentence going before and following after, and is marked thus **;**

 A **comma** is a distinction of an imperfect sentence wherein…the sentence following is included and is noted with this shorter semicircle **,**

A **pause** is a distinction of a sentence, though perfect in itself, yet joined to another, being marked with two pricks **:**

A **period** is the distinction of a sentence, in all respects perfect, and is marked with one full prick over against the lower part of the last letter.

If a sentence be with an **interrogation**, we use this note **?** *Ben Jonson 1640*

1640 CE

In this poem Jonson ridicules an 'idiot' laughing in the wrong places by misunderstanding the 'points' (punctuation):

Groome Ideot

Ideot, last night, I prayd thee but forbeare
To read my verses; now I must to heare:
For offring, with thy smiles, my wit to grace,
Thy ignorance still laughs in the wrong place.
And so my sharpnesse thou no lesse [disjoints],
Then thou didst late my sense, loosing my points.
So [have] I seene at [Christmas] sports one lost,
And, hood-winkd, for a man, embrace a post

1665 CE

First English Newspaper

Despite popularity in Europe, printing regulations prevented news periodicals from being printed in England until the publisher Nathaniel Butter was granted permission to publish the Corante in 1621. He went on to publish The Weekly News and established what would eventually become the newspaper industry.

Not everyone approved. The theatre had become an authority in itself, capable of shaping and influencing public opinion. The playwright and first Poet Laureate, Ben Jonson was an angry opponent to the new medium and he satirised Nathaniel Butter in his play 'The Staple of News':

> *The very printing of 'em makes them news;*
>
> *That have not the heart to believe any thing,*
>
> *But what they see in print.*

English Grammar

Three years after his death, Ben Jonson's work 'English Grammar' was published. It provided guidance on punctuation including reference to the colon as 'two pricks'. Jonson was so fond of the two-pricks he used them in his name *(see page 66)*.

Oxford Gazette

The oldest surviving English newspaper, the Oxford Gazette *(known today as the London Gazette)*, started when King Charles II relocated to Oxford to avoid the plague. Royal Courtiers were unwilling to touch newspapers from London at the time.

The Lexicographer

Frustrated at the inconsistency of the printed language, a group of book sellers commissioned Samuel Johnson to create an English Dictionary.

After nine years labour, Johnson completed his work in which he noted:

> *Language is only the instrument of science, and words are but the signs of ideas: I wish, however, that the instrument might be less apt to decay, and that signs might be permanent, like the things which they denote.*

With over 40,000 words, detailed notes and literary quotations, Johnson's dictionary became the most popular authority for the English language. The influence of his work extended beyond Britain into Europe and America and the style and content of his dictionary informed and influenced future dictionaries including the Oxford English Dictionary that today claims to be the definitive record of the English language (not all agree with the claim).

The Icon of Prescriptivism

Robert Lowth published his Short Introduction to the English Language in 1762 and so began the 'prescriptive grammar' movement — English was to be a language with rules of writing (that many would happily ignore).

Over 200 publications on English grammar and language were published between 1750 and 1800. Sales of red ink boomed.

Different dialects meant different spelling and grammar, and in the absence an authoritative dictionary, people could in any case choose to spell words as they wished.

Samuel Johnson tried to use what he considered to be the most logical choices when selecting the spellings to use for his dictionary entries. In the same way that printers word choices had lasting impacts on written English, so did Samuel Johnson's decisions, for example he mistakenly spelled 'ake' as 'ache'.

Some of his descriptions have a personal bias, not least his description of a 'patron' that reflects his thoughts on the Earl of Chesterfield who provided patronage for Johnson's dictionary:

COLON: A point [:] used to mark a pause greater than that of a comma, and less than that of a period. Its use is not very exactly fixed, nor is it very necessary, being confounded by most with the semicolon. It was used before punctuation was refined, to mark almost any sense less than a period.

BEDPRESSER: A heavy lazy fellow

JOGGER: One who moves heavily and dully.

LEXICOGRAPHER: A writer of dictionaries; a harmless drudge that busies himself in tracing the original, and detailing the signification of words.

OATS: A grain, which in England is generally given to horses, but in Scotland appears to support the people.

PARENTHESIS: A sentence so included in another sentence, as that it may be taken out, without injuring the sense of that which incloses it: being commonly marked thus, ()

PATRON: One who countenances, supports or protects. Commonly a wretch, who supports with insolence, and is paid with flattery.

'J' and 'U', missing from Ben Jonson's work 150 years earlier are included in Samuel Johnson's dictionary.

'X' is included too but with a note explaining it is 'a letter, which, though found in Saxon words, begins no word in the English language'.

The French Dictionnarre had been entrusted to 40 scholars who took over 50 years to complete it. L'Académie française is today made up of 40 members known as les immortels and is the definitive authority for the French language.

In contrast English has no official authority. Therefore however prescriptive grammarians may have been, there has never been a truly 'correct' version of written English.

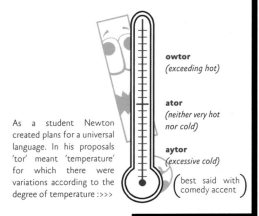

owtor
(exceeding hot)

ator
(neither very hot nor cold)

aytor
(excessive cold)

(best said with)
(comedy accent)

As a student Newton created plans for a universal language. In his proposals 'tor' meant 'temperature' for which there were variations according to the degree of temperature :>>>

Newton Sees the Light

Isaac Newton's 'Opticks' was his first published work in English. Previously Newton and his scientific peers had published their works in Latin.

English now became the language of science. and was gifted new words like 'gravity', 'electricity' and 'thermometer'. Today English is regarded as the international language of science and nearly all scientific articles are published in English.

Robert Raikes used his newspaper, the Gloucester Journal, to publicise his schools. His stories were picked up by other publications too:

Young people lately more neglected than the cattle in the field... were here seen cleanly, quiet, observant of order, submissive, courteous in behaviour, and in conversation free from that vileness which marks our wretched vulgar.

The children had been bred up in total ignorance... These children have no teaching but on the Sunday; what they learn at the leisure hours in the week is the effect of their own desire to improve.—Many have books at their looms, to seize any vacant minute, when their work is retarded by the breaking of threads.

The Gentleman's Magazine, 1787

Teaching the Slums

Newspaper owner, Robert Raikes, established schools to teach reading and writing to children that were working in factories. Raikes believed the schools would help children in the slums of Gloucester avoid a life of crime. Their six day working week meant the children could only attend on a Sunday. In less than ten years, over a quarter of a million children attended a Sunday School.

Louis-Nicolas Robert was awarded a patent for his paper making machine in 1799. He entrusted development to his English brother-in-law, John Gamble, away from the difficulties of the French Revolution.

Gamble agreed to share Robert's patent with the brothers, Sealy and Henry Fourdrinier. The Fourdrinier brothers subsequently obtained new patents of their own.

Louis-Nicolas retired from paper making and finished his life as a poorly paid teacher in post-revolution France. He died in poverty.

The costs of the invention caused the Fourdrinier brothers to become bankrupt although the family did eventually receive an income from their investment.

The Fourdrinier machine is still used today.

Forward Rolls

A former French soldier, Louis-Nicolas Robert invented what would become the 'Fourdrinier machine' in 1798. It made continuous rolls of paper, and along with other inventions during the Industrial Revolution, helped significantly speed up the printing and distribution of the written word.

The Industrial Revolution drew people into cities and surrounded them with words in newspapers, books, documents and on signs and posters. More people were writing and reading in more and more ways.

Pepper & Salt it as You Please

'Lord' Dexter was an American eccentric. An uneducated but accidentally successful man, he was the source of resentment from others who would give him bad advice in the hope of ruining him.

He attempted to sell bed pans (for warming beds) to the West Indies. People bought them to use for cooking and he made a profit.

He was advised to ship coal to Newcastle (a city built on the coal industry). His ship happened to arrive during a miners strike and he made another profit.

Late in life, to the disgust of his neighbours, he tried to spend as much money as possible. He converted a huge house into a museum and invited anyone to visit.

He wrote a book of ramblings that included descriptions of his museum, his views on the nature of the devil, his marital difficulties and the planning of bridges.

One thing that didn't appear in his book was punctuation — not a single punctuation mark!

His book proved so popular it was reprinted. For the second edition he added one page full of punctuation marks for readers to 'pepper and salt it as they please'.

A Pickle For The Knowing Ones went on to be reprinted for sale eight times over the next 200 years and is now considered as a classic of American literature.

The printed word increasingly surrounded people

Newspapers reported news from across the expanding British Empire including the adventures of great explorers like David Livingstone writing from Africa.

Printers experimented with typography to create posters promoting goods, events and political activities.

A

PICKLE FOR THE KNOWING ONES

BY

LORD TIMOTHY DEXTER

fouder mister printer the Nowing ones complane of my book the fust edition had no stops I put in A Nuf here and thay may peper and solt it as they plese

,,,,,,,,,,,,,,,,,,,,,,,,,,,,,,,,,,,,
,,,,,,,,,,,,,,,,,,,,,,,,,,,,,,,,,,,,
,,,,,,,,,,,,,,,,,,,,,,,,,,,,,,,,,,,,
,,,,,,,,,,,,,,,,,,,,,,,,,,,,,,,,,,,,
,,,,,,,,,,,,,,,,,,,,,,,,,,,,,,,,,,,,
,,,,,,,,,,,,,,,,,,,,,,,,,,,,,,,,,,,,
,,,,,,,,,,,,,,,,,,,,,,,,,,,,,,,,,,,,
,,,,,,,,,,,,,,,,,,,,,,,,,,,,,,,,,,,,
,,,,,,,,,,,,,,,,,,,,,,,,,,,,,,,,,,,,

....
....
....
....
....
....
....

....
....
....
....
....

?????????????????????????????????????
?????????????????????????????????????
?????????????????????????????????????
?????????????????????????????????????

!!!!!!!!!!!!!!!!!!!!!!!!!!!!!!!!!!!!
!!!!!!!!!!!!!!!!!!!!!!!!!!!!!!!!!!!!
!!!!!!!!!!!!!!!!!!!!!!!!!!!!!!!!!!!!
!!!!!!!!!!!!!!!!!!!!!!!!!!!!!!!!!!!!

,,,,,,,,,,,,,,,,,,,,,,,,,,,,,,,,,,,,
,,,,,,,,,,,,,,,,,,,,,,,,,,,,,,,,,,,,
,,,,,,,,,,,,,,,,,,,,,,,,,,,,,,,,,,,,
,,,,,,,,,,,,,,,,,,,,,,,,,,,,,,,,,,,,

....
....
....
....

1855 CE

—*In the briefest correspondence known, only two figures were used; the first contained a note of interrogation (?), implying "Is there any news?" The answer was a cypher(o), "None."*

The Hampshire Advertiser, 1851

SEND MESSAGE STOP.

Early telegrams required Samuel Morse's code to be decoded by skilled operators until David Edward Hughes developed a system in 1855 that printed text.

Messages were charged by the word and so were brief and to the point and punctuation was often omitted. Famously 'STOP' was used in place of a period (we used to call them periods in England too).

```
          HOW TO WRITE TELEGRAMS PROPERLY
If  it  seems  impossible  to  convey
your  meaning  clearly  without  the  use
of  punctuation,  use  may  be  made  of
the  celebrated  word  "stop,"  which  is
known  the  world  over  as  the  official
telegraphic    or    cable    word    for
"period."
This  word  "stop"  may  have  perplexed
you  the  first  time  you  encountered
it  in  a  message.  Use  of  this  word  in
telegraphic  communications  was  greatly
increased  during  the  World  War,  when
the  Government  employed  it  widely  as
a  precaution  against  having  messages
garbled  or  misunderstood,  as  a  result
of  the  misplacement  or  emission  of  the
tiny  dot  or  period.
                          Nelson E. Ross, 1928
```

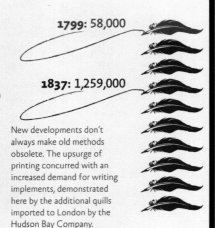

Quills Imported

1799: 58,000

1837: 1,259,000

New developments don't always make old methods obsolete. The upsurge of printing concurred with an increased demand for writing implements, demonstrated here by the additional quills imported to London by the Hudson Bay Company.

1878 CE

QWERTY

In 1878 Christopher Scholes patented his type-writing machine. The QWERTY keyboard on typewriters used limited keys to reduce costs and space. There was no space for "curly quotes" or exclamation marks!

On typewriters straight quotes, used for indicating feet and inches, were also used as quotation marks.

A typist could type an exclamation mark by typing an apostrophe and then a backspace to type a dot beneath the apostrophe.

With only a hyphen available, a dash was indicated by use of a double hyphen.

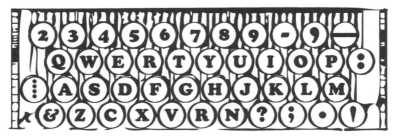

The King's English

By the twentieth century, Primary education was no longer restricted to Sundays in between factory shifts. It had become compulsory for all children in the UK. Increased education, increased literacy and increased teaching led to a lot more debate about punctuation.

As ever not everybody agreed on how to punctuate, but plenty believed their way to be the best way and in 1906 the Fowler brothers published the 'King's English' in which they advocated, in an ironically lengthy and long winded way, the use of 'light punctuation'.

Henry Fowler went on to write 'A Dictionary of Modern English' in 1926 and Winston Churchill directed his staff to read it. As a man that advocated whipping for the ignorance of English, they no doubt studied hard.

The Exclamation Arrives!!

The Exclamation mark finally made it onto typewriter keyboards in 1970.

queen@royal.gov.uk

Queen Elizabeth II sent her first email in 1976. Ray Tomlinson the inventor of this new way of sending messages had sent the first ever email himself five years earlier.

Having been absent from typewriters, the Exclamation Mark made up for lost time by demanding attention on email subject headings across the world!!!!!

Ironic Brevity........

It is a sound principle that as few stops should be used as will do the work... all that is printed should have as many stops as to help the reader, and not more.

Any one who finds himself putting down several commas close to one another should reflect that he is making himself disagreeable, and question his conscience, as severely as we ought to do about disagreeable conduct in real life, whether it is necessary.

The King's English, 1906, Henry Watson Fowler and Francis George Fowler

During his time as a school master Henry Fowler was nicknamed 'Joey Stinker'

" Naturally I am biased in favour of boys learning English. I would make them all learn English: and then I would let the clever ones learn Latin as an honour, and Greek as a treat. But the only thing I would whip them for would be not knowing English. I would whip them hard for that. "
Winston Churchill

The @-sign is not a punctuation mark but a symbol representing the word 'at'. usage dates back at least as far as the 16th century and historically it was used in commerce eg. '4 apples @ 20p'.

It found its way on to typewriters long before the exclamation mark but became most famous after Ray Tomlinson chose to use it in his first email when he identified himself as
tomlinson@bbn-tenexa

Despite its age it has become a symbol of modern communications.

1982 CE

Personal Computing

The Commodore 64 became the best ever selling personal computer and thrust punctuation into a new role of supporting painstakingly typed codes for computer games.

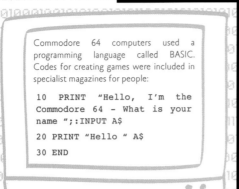

Commodore 64 computers used a programming language called BASIC. Codes for creating games were included in specialist magazines for people:

```
10  PRINT "Hello, I'm the
Commodore 64 - What is your
name ";:INPUT A$
20 PRINT "Hello " A$
30 END
```

The Apple Macintosh followed in 1984 and personal computers quickly became essential to business, education and home life. Computers allowed vast freedom for presenting information with new fonts and symbols and the software to create even more. Anybody could become a printer and publisher.

1991 CE

world wide web

While English is the most widely used language on the internet, other languages are expanding rapidly as infrastructures develop throughout the world.

Current estimates are that while about a quarter of people online are English users, over half of online content is in English.

Historical English documents are also available online, meaning technology simultaneously leads to new forms of written English while also preserving former versions of the language.

Tim Berners-Lee's creation was released into the public domain in 1991. Four years later Microsoft's Internet Explorer allowed people to access information and communicate across the world and English became the language of the internet and adopted new words and new meanings like geeks, trolls and lols.

1992 CE

C u l8tr!!! :)

Modern writing often uses the rapid exchange of messages and a more conversational style has emerged in which punctuation marks have meaning in their own right!!!!!!!!

In **1995** users sent an average of **4 text messages** a month. 15 years later **193,000** texts were sent **every second!**

Vodafone sent the first SMS text message in the UK in 1992. Like telegrams 150 years earlier, the limitation on characters that could be sent in a message meant that punctuation was often dispensed of in favour of brevity.

However punctuation marks took on a new role as 'emoticons' and though once considered appropriate only for informal use, they have arguably become a new form of punctuation :)

Ellipsis:
Dramatic,
likes to tease

Apostrophe:
Quiet &
secretive

Comma:
Busy, likes to be
active. Hates
disorganisation

Speech Marks:
Chatty, love to gossip

Colon:
Talkative. Likes to
make announcements

Curvy Brackets:
Caring & nurturing,
helpful to others

Question Mark:
Inquisitive,
unsure, needs
reassurance

Exclamation:
Excitable,
dramatic,
loves attention

Slash:
Indecisive,
easily confused

Semicolon:
Easily bored
& distracted

Square Brackets:
Nerdy, full of
information

Dashes:
Enjoy new
opportunities & making connections

Full Stop:
Blunt, bossy,
firm, clear

~ FULL STOP ~

●

Other Names: Period, Point, Interpunct, Dot

Best Known For: Ending sentences.

Other Uses:

   ❧ Indicating an abbreviated word: etc.

   ❧ Indicating a decimal point: 2.1

   ❧ After initials for names: Mr W. G. Smith

   ❧ Website addresses: www.monsterpunctuation.co.uk

FULL STOP

.

Interesting Stuff:

During the 3rd Century BCE a Greek scholar called Aristophanes used a system of dots called distinctiones during to indicate how a reader should breathe when reading passages of text:

A distinctio point (top level) **(˙)** indicated a very long passage
(known as periodos) (Take a deep breath!)

A subdistinctio dot (base level) **(.)** indicated a longer passage
(known as a colon)

A media distinctio dot (mid level) **(·)** indicated a short passage
(known as a komma)

Although never widely used during his lifetime, Aristophanes' system features in a guide to grammar written nearly a thousand years later by Isodore of Seville.

The Romans sometimes used vertically centred dots (or triangles) known as 'interpuncts' between words to separate them.

ROMAN·STYLE·INTERPUNCTS

Also known as 'space dots' or 'middle' or 'centred' dots, interpuncts were commonly used to indicate decimal points until they were replaced by full stops after the introduction of typewriters and calculators.

Prior to the 20th century the term 'period' was referred to in both British and American usage (the term 'full stop' was only used in reference to a period used to end a sentence). During the 20th century the British began to refer to all punctuation dots as 'full-stops' while in the US they continued with the traditional term.

Dots (or points) are the most frequently used of all punctuation marks. Up to about the 16th century English punctuation was referred to as 'pointing'.

Space

Other Names: Gap, Whitespace, Blank

Best Known For: Separating characters, words and paragraphs.

Space

Interesting Stuff:

The oldest western texts used dots and lines to separate words until the Greek style of writing continuously without word dividers or spaces, known as 'scriptio continua', became the preferred style from about 200CE.

Space is used as a word divider

DOTS·CAN·ALSO·BE·USED·AND ARE·KNOWN·AS·INTERPUNCTS

SOMETIMES:INTERPUNCTS:ARE DOUBLE:OR:TREBLE:DOTS

Vertical|lines|can|be|seen|as|word dividers|on|some|ancient|inscriptions

Early religious texts were intended to be read aloud and the words were memorised in advance by readers who only used the writing as a prompt. Readability was less critical than the cost of writing space.

Texts were copied by hand and as the Bible spread to new countries and new languages it was common for scribes to add their own guidance notes and marks to help readers understand how to read text written in an unfamiliar language (usually Latin).

A 'hypodiastole' (above) was used in some Ancient Greek texts to assist with word separation. A hyphen indicated two words to be read as one word, while a hypodiastole indicated the opposite — two words that might be confused as one word but that should be separated.

A slightly curved version of the hyphen could also be used and is known as an enotikon or 'tie'.

Irish scribes are credited with beginning the practise of using 'white space' to separate words and word separation can be seen from about 600CE. It became common practice across Europe by the 11th century.

The use of spaces to separate words, enabled words to be recognised not just by the letterforms within a word, but also by the overall shape of the word itself.

Fluid readers are thought to recognise words most easily by focussing on the centre of the word. The use of space to distinguish words has made this process clearer and quicker, allowing us to read texts very quickly.

Although not a punctuation mark, space is one of the oldest and most important aspects of our punctuation system.

Many modern email and website addresses use a form of scriptio continua today:

www.monsterpunctuation.co.uk

WHITE
space

✳ **Question Mark** ✳

Other Names: Interrogation Mark, Query

Best Known For: Indicating a direct question

Other Uses: Alongside an exclamation mark as an expression of disbelief or excitement (known as an 'interrobang')

Question Mark

?

Interesting Stuff:

The Question Mark may derive from the Latin word 'quaestiō' meaning 'question'.

Possible evolution from word to punctuation mark:

quaestiō

A symbol called 'punctus interrogativus' was used as early as the 8th century to indicate the end of a question but wasn't widely used.

punctus interrogativus

There have been proposals to create alternate versions of the question mark including the 'irony mark' to indicate irony or sarcasm.

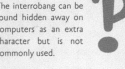

An 'irony mark'

An 'interrobang' can be used to represent a question asked in an excited manner and to express excitement/disbelief or to ask a rhetorical question. Although the symbol isn't widely used, many people combine question marks and exclamation marks for the same purpose!!?!

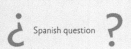

The interrobang can be found hidden away on computers as an extra character but is not commonly used.

An inverted question mark is used in Spanish writing to begin a question (a normal question mark closes the question).

Spanish question

In Greek writing a semicolon is used as a question mark.

The Greek question mark is the same as a semicolon.

An upside-down and reversed semicolon looks similar to a question mark. This same shape used to be known as a 'punctus elavatus' and was used by some writers to indicate a pause that was longer than a semicolon but shorter than a full stop.

Exclamation Mark

Other Names: Bang, Pling

Best Known For: Emphasising a statement and indicating emotion

Other Uses: ⚡ On signs to indicate a warning

⚡ Between parentheses to indicate sarcasm (!)

⚡ As an interrobang *(see page 36)*

Exclamation Mark
!

Interesting Stuff:

Some scribes used the medieval equivalent to 'hooray!' after relevant sentences, written as 'io' (Latin for 'joy').

The exclamation mark possibly evolved from the Latin into its modern form:

$$ IO \quad \overset{I}{O} \quad ! $$

During the 15th century English printers called it the 'Note of Admiration'. It was used in King Edward VI's 'Catechism' printed in 1533 but wasn't widely used until very recently!

Modern printers have given it various names including the 'screamer', 'startler', 'gasper', 'slammer' and the BANG! More recently computer programmers have named it as a 'pling'!

It is used as a symbol of caution and can be found on street signs and product labels in many countries!

There have long been arguments about the use of the exclamation as a punctuation mark with some publishers banning any use of it. Many advocate for it to be used sparingly and consider its impact to be diminished by overuse!!

Today it is widely used in informal communications and sometimes considered as a message in itself !!!!!!!!!!

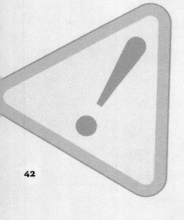

Curved Brackets

( )

Other Names: Parentheses, Soft Brackets, Round Brackets

Best Known For: Including information that is useful but is not a direct part of the sentence.

Other Uses:
1) A single bracket is sometimes used in an ordered list (such as this list)

2) Providing additional information about something or somebody
   eg. Mr Smith (the teacher)

3) As part of a 'smiley' :-)

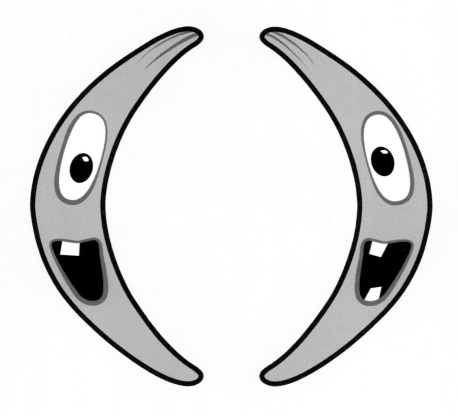

Curved Brackets

( )

Interesting Stuff:

Parenthesis (the singular of parentheses) derives from Greek meaning "to put beside", and this is how they are most commonly used in writing (as an aside).

They took various forms in medieval writing before becoming the crescent shape we are familiar with today. The Renaissance writer, Erasmus, referred to them as 'lunulae' (little moons).

Their other name (Brackets) is taken from the French word 'braguette' meaning 'codpiece'. Cod has nothing to do with fish, instead it meant 'scrotum', and the cod-piece is the part of trousers that joins the legs together.

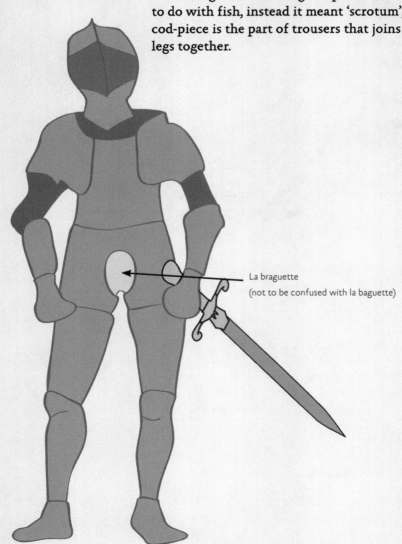

La braguette
(not to be confused with la baguette)

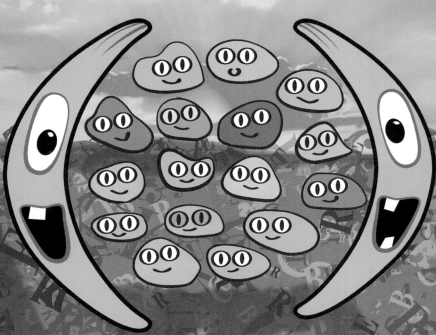

CURVED BRACKETS

(Useful information)

Dashes

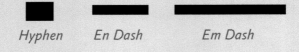

Hyphen   En Dash   Em Dash

Names: Hyphen, En Dash, Em Dash

Best Known For: Connecting things

Uses: Strictly a hyphen is distinct from dashes. The distinctions are:

+ A **hyphen** connects words and joins parts of words across sentences

+ An **en dash** connects numbers and dates

+ An **em dash** connects thoughts, breaks sentences and can be used for attributing quotes

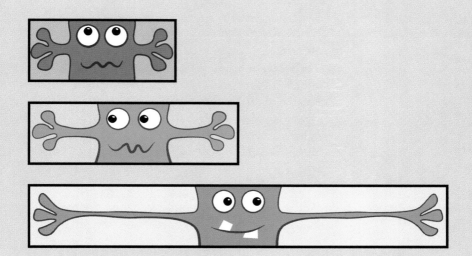

Dashes

Interesting Stuff:

▬ **hyphen**
(connects words)

▬▬ **en dash**
(connects numbers)

▬▬▬ **em dash**
(connects thoughts)

▬ **minus sign**
(mathematical symbol)

▬▬ **underscore**

The underscore is derived from the typewriter and was used to underline words

Gutenberg actually used two lines for a hyphen (rather than the single line used today). People had used dashes long before printing, however all modern day punctuation has been shaped by the invention of the printing press as printers have sought to find ways to overcome technical challenges and to make text as readable as possible.

To save space early typewriters did not have dashes -- typists therefore represented a dash by use of a double-hyphen.

The German Printer, Johannes Gutenberg is credited for inventing the modern hyphen during the 15th century, although it appeared in England at least 200 years earlier and is one of the oldest punctuation marks having been used during Ancient Greek texts *(see the hypodiastole page 34)*

Gutenberg invented a 'movable type' printing system that started a printing revolution in Europe in 1450. His method of printing required letters to be held in place within a frame — meaning each line of text had to be the same length. He used hyphens at the end of sentences to indicate that a word continued on the next line and to ensure every line could be of equal length and so fit within the frame for the printing press.

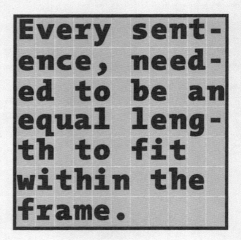

'Dashes' came into use during the 18th century.

En dashes *(used for joining numbers)* are (roughly) the width of a letter 'N' and em dashes *(used for joining thoughts)* are the width of a letter 'M'.

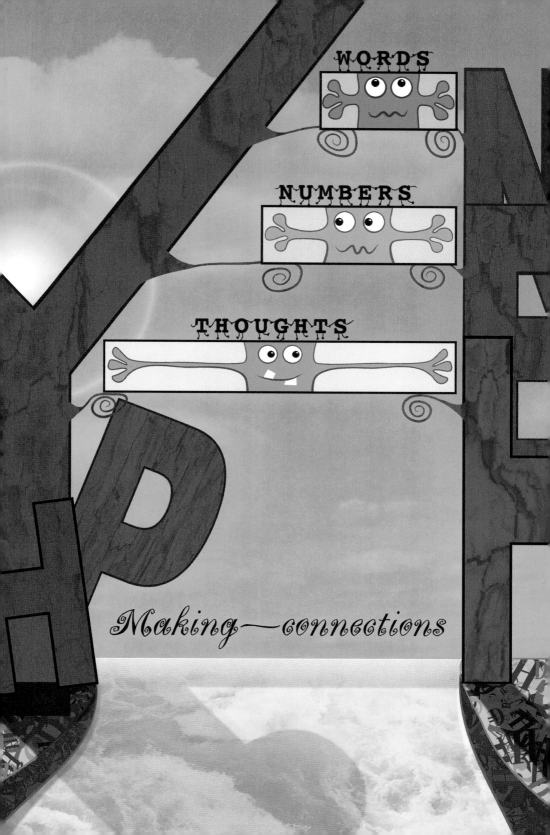

Semicolon

;

Other names: Super-Comma, Comma-Colon, Wink

Best Known For: Connecting independent (but related) parts
of a sentence

Other Uses: Separating items within lists

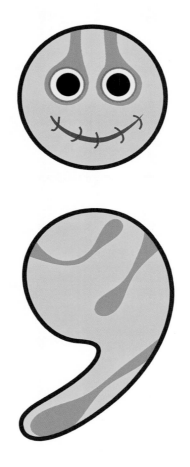

Semicolon

;

Interesting Stuff:

A semicolon is still used as a question mark in Greek writing (see page 38)

THE SEMICOLON MOVEMENT

The semicolon is used as a symbol by 'The Semicolon Movement' to represent hope for people who self-harm:

The semicolon is used when a sentence could have ended, but didn't

Members across the world use the semicolon in posters, photographs and as body art and tattoos.

There are various anecdotes of the semicolon causing confusion in legal texts including this account of a duel between two French professors. The placement of the colon and semicolon suggest either a reporter with a dark sense of humour or more likely that it was a literary joke rather than an account of real events::

.—A duel, with small swords, lately took place in Paris, between two well known jurisconsults of the law-school on account of a passage of the Pandects. The one who contended that the passage in question ought to be concluded by a semicolon was wounded in the arm: his adversary maintained that it should be a colon; and quoted , in support of his opinion, the text of Trebonius.

The Family Magazine, 1837

The semicolon as a symbol began life as a question mark in Ancient Greek.

Modern usage is thanks to the Italian printer, Aldus Manutius who is credited with printing the first semicolon in 1494; it took the best part of another century before it was regularly used in Britain.

The literal meaning of 'semi-colon' is 'part of a colon'; it has been referred to as a 'comma-colon' and a 'super-comma' and described as representing a pause shorter than a full-stop but lengthier than a comma.

Manutius apparently used it to divide words of opposed meanings and to enable rapid changes of direction within sentences; he isn't thought to have used them as winking smileys ;-)

The semicolon has been controversial both with regard to usage and even whether it needs to be used at all; some claim that it is only needed in poorly constructed sentences and can be better represented by other marks (such as the dash, comma and full-stop).

> *"[The semicolon is] a parasite, a timid, fainthearted, insipid thing, denoting merely uncertainty, a lack of audacity, a fuzziness of thought"*
>
> François Cavanna, French Author

For others it is regarded with admiration; an expression of a writers finesse or in the words of a former president: 'a useful little chap'...

> *"With educated people, I suppose, punctuation is a matter of rules; with me it is a matter of feeling. But I must say I have a great respect for the semi-colon; it's a useful little chap."*
>
> Abraham Lincoln, President of the United States

In modern use the semicolon has come to represent a wink ;)

Two parts; of the same journey

Speech Marks

6699

Other names: Quotation Marks, Inverted Commas, Double Quotes, Curly Quotes, Book Quotes

Best Known For: Enclosing text that indicates direct speech

Other Uses: *(Usage is the same for single and double quotation marks)*

❯ Indicating irony or a purposefully unusual usage of a word ('Scare Quotes')

❯ Indicating a title: 'Monster Punctuation'

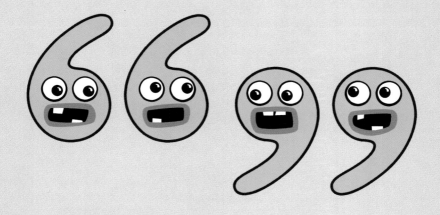

Speech Marks

" "

Interesting Stuff:

Straight quotes (known as a 'prime' and 'double prime' symbol) are used for indicating measurements in feet and inches.

« In French 'guillemets' are used instead of quotation marks. They are named after the 16th century printer, Guillaume Le Bé. »

US-English is not necessarily 'new'. Many words that we consider to be American (such as 'diaper') are old English words that dropped out of fashion in Britain but continued to be used in the US.

Americanisms are foreign words, and should be so treated... I gesse is favourite expression of Chaucer's... But though it is good old English, it is not good new English... we have it not from Chaucer, but from the Yankees..
The King's English, 1906

The printing press and smaller book formats led to a popular new format for reading "the novel" and stories littered with speech needed a new method of punctuation.

Quotations and speech have been (and still are) represented in many ways *including distinguishing text with different typefaces.*

" In the early 16th century German printers used
" double commas in the left hand margin (like those
" to the left of this paragraph) to indicate speech. This
" followed earlier practices of scribes who used various
" marks within margins to draw attention to
" particular text.

" *An early style of indicating speech was to include*
" *a quotation mark on every line of the quoted speech.*
" *This was replaced by using opening and closing*
" *quotations but the indent where the quotation marks*
" *previously appeared on each line was left. This is*
" *why quotes are often indented within a paragraph.*

There continued to be variations in methods for expressing quotation marks until the modern practise was widely adopted in the 19th century. Even then there continued to be a variation between the British-English style of using 'single quotes' to indicate direct speech and the US style of using "double quotation" marks. Today the choice of using either is a matter of 'style' or "preference".

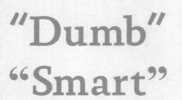

Arranging type to be visually appealing and understandable is known as 'typography'. Typographers refer to straight quotes as 'dumb quotes' and curly quotes as 'smart quotes'.

The use of straight quotes is a legacy from the limited keys available on a typewriter.

SPEECH MARKS

"Indicating speech"

Apostrophe

,

Best Known For: Indicating a missing letter (or letters)

Other Uses: ❧ To show possession eg. Sarah's book

❧ To indicate a term is plural (but not when it would be considered a 'Grocer's Apostrophe')

Apostrophe

,

(Barely) Interesting Stuff:

The French, who are credited with inventing them, like to use more than one apostrophe in every sentence compared to English usage of about one in every twenty sentences.

Apple's

In most cases an apostrophe is not needed to indicate a word is plural:

cats	not	cat's
photos	not	photo's
oranges	not	orange's

Using an unnecessary 'plural apostrophe' became known as a 'Grocer's Apostrophe' during the 20th century after campaigners highlighted handwritten signs such as *Two pound's of Apple's* as an example of what they referred to as the 'decline of modern English'.

As with quotation marks the limited keys available on typewriters led to prime marks being used in place of the curly shape of an apostrophe.

Given their simple appearance, apostrophes attract a bizarre level of interest. There are websites, societies and campaigns dedicated to them, many delighting in highlighting 'incorrect' usage.

The French printer Geoffroy Tory is credited with inventing them during the early 16th century, although Aldus Manutius used them in his works as early as 1501 *(see page 19)*. English printers adopted the French practice of using them as a mark of elision. At the time there were many English words like 'loved' that ended with a silent 'e'. By replacing the unsounded letters, printers were better able to fit lines of text neatly through the printing press.

A couple of hundred years later people began sticking apostrophes into words to indicate possession. The placement of a small squiggle could now entirely change the meaning of a sentence:

> *The girl's toys*
>
> *The girls' toys*

In modern times it's common to see shop signs that dispense completely with apostrophes:

> *Girls Toys*

Apostrophes are regularly omitted by people exchanging messages on phones and like the semicolon *(page 52)* there are ongoing arguments about the need for apostrophes.

And so the usage (or abusage) of the apostrophe continues to evolve and adapt, leading to some of the dullest most tedious debates ev'r.

Colon

:

Best Known For: Introducing an idea or a list.

Other Uses:

❧ To mark a ratio (50:1)

❧ As a divider between titles and names eg. Treasure Island: Robert Louis Stevenson

❧ Dividing hours and minutes (18:30)

❧ To indicate dialogue:

Actor 1: "Why hello!"
Actor 2: "Oh there you are..."

Colon

Interesting Stuff:

In its earliest form the colon wasn't a punctuation mark: Instead it referred to a passage of text that was longer than a 'comma' and shorter than a 'period' and known as a 'kolon' *(see page 30)*. Marking a colon was originally indicated by a low dot.

When the mark took the form of two dots is unknown but William Caxton used the modern form of a colon within his books as early as the late 15th century: Caxton's usage and meaning of the marks he used were inconsistent and it took another hundred years or so before people began to agree on the purpose of a colon, described in 1616 as:

> *"A marke of a sentence not fully ended which is made with two prickes."*
>
> John Bullokar (1616) An English Expositor

The playwright, Ben Jonson referred to the colon in a similar way a few years later in his book *The English Grammar*:

> *"A pause is a distinction of a sentence, though perfect in itself, yet joined to another, being marked thus with two pricks (:)."*

He liked the two pricks so much he placed them between his names for his signature:

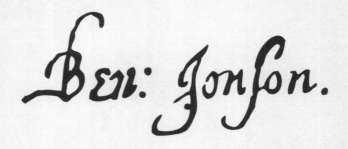

CC *What a quantity of useless controversial stuff has been written upon the "proper" use of the semicolon and colon!*

[At last] the public settled the business by throwing their two favourite stops overboard. The schoolmasters, however, picked them up, and are still striving to keep them afloat... **"**

Justin Brenan
Composition and Punctuation, 1865

Brenan considered the colon to be superfluous and described it as having been 'literally dashed to pieces' and superseded by the dash.

The colon survived: arguments about punctuation survived too.

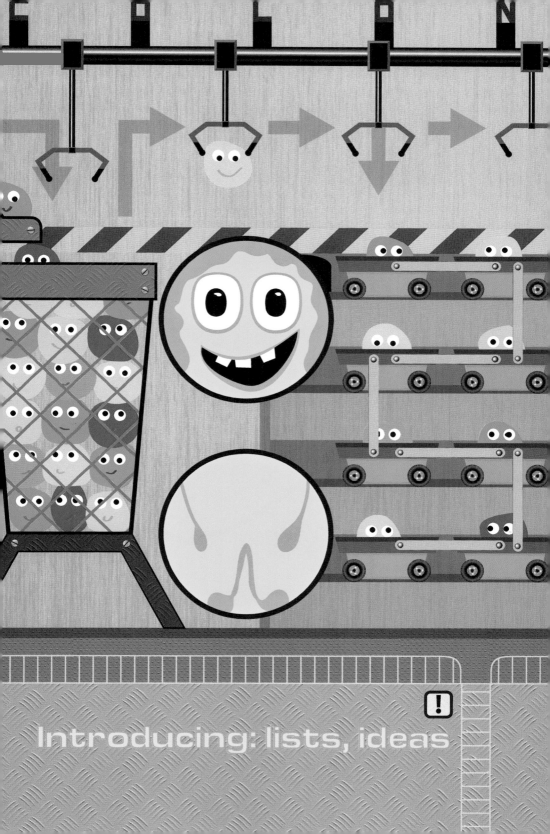

Introducing: lists, ideas

Comma

,

Best Known For: Separating things

Other Uses: People have contrived impressive lists of 'rules' and ways for a comma to separate things, but essentially that's all it really does — separates things!

Comma

,

Interesting Stuff:

Like the identically shaped apostrophe, the comma has managed to attract a curious level of complexity.

Suggested functions of the comma include:

- To separate nonrestrictive modifiers
- To separate appositives that are not essential to the meaning of the sentence
- To separate adverbs and short parentheticals that are not essential to the meaning of the sentence

The Greek scholar Aristophanes *(page 30)* could never have envisioned such complexity when he first used a dot to represent a 'komma' (a short passage of text) during the 3rd century BCE.

Back then, it was an indicator, for the reader to know, a short breath, would be needed. For many years the comma continued to be used to indicate a short breath, or pause. This understanding prevails today, despite that modern punctuation is intended for the comprehension of text, rather than for reading aloud.

When the comma first appeared in print during the 15th century / it was not in its current form / but was instead shaped as a virgule (a forward slash) and some writers would indicate a longer pause with a double virgule //

The Italian printer, Aldus Manutius, moved the virgule to a lower position and curved it slightly to become the modern 'comma' (Latin for 'short phrase') *(see page 16)*.

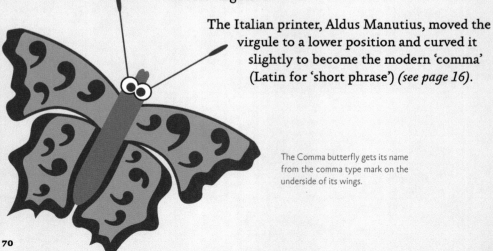

The Comma butterfly gets its name from the comma type mark on the underside of its wings.

Separating, organising

Ellipsis

● ● ●

Other names: Suspension Point, Dot-Dot-Dot

Best Known For: indicating a sentence is intentionally incomplete

Other Uses:
- Indicating an unfinished thought
- Indicating a lengthy pause
- In place of text that has been removed because it is considered unnecessary
- In place of sections of quotes that have been removed or not included
- To build suspense or anticipation

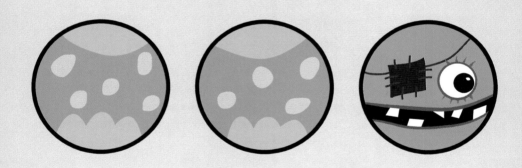

Ellipsis

• • •

Interesting Stuff:

● ● ● ● ●

An ellipsis is commonly accepted to be made up of three dots and some will insist that it should always be three dots, and only three dots..

However in modern use the number of dots used have come to be considered as a meaning in itself........!

Lots of dots may be interpreted as excited or impatient, while less dots may be more blunt

The word 'ellipsis' derives from an Ancient Greek word meaning 'omission' or 'too fall short'. The practise of omitting information that a reader can work out for themselves is ancient and common to many languages. Ellipses were used in the Viking language Old Norse and more recently in Shakespeare's works, however... these refer to the structure of language and not the usage of three dots to represent the ellipsis as a punctuation mark.

In mathematics 'ellipsis' refers to an angle 'falling short'... the use of the term for writing was taken from the mathematical term after it first appeared in print as a punctuation mark at the end of the 16th century.

It developed into the modern format during the 17th century and has since evolved to represent not only omission... but a sense of mystery, expectation, dramatic.. pause and guess-what-happens-next...

Historically an ellipsis in British-English was just two dots but today 'authorities' proclaim the rule is that an ellipsis consists of exactly three dots. A rule happily ignored on excited emails and text messages across the world............

A long time ago in a galaxy far, far away....

Each Star Wars film begins with the above text. Some use an ellipsis with.... four dots and some use... just three!

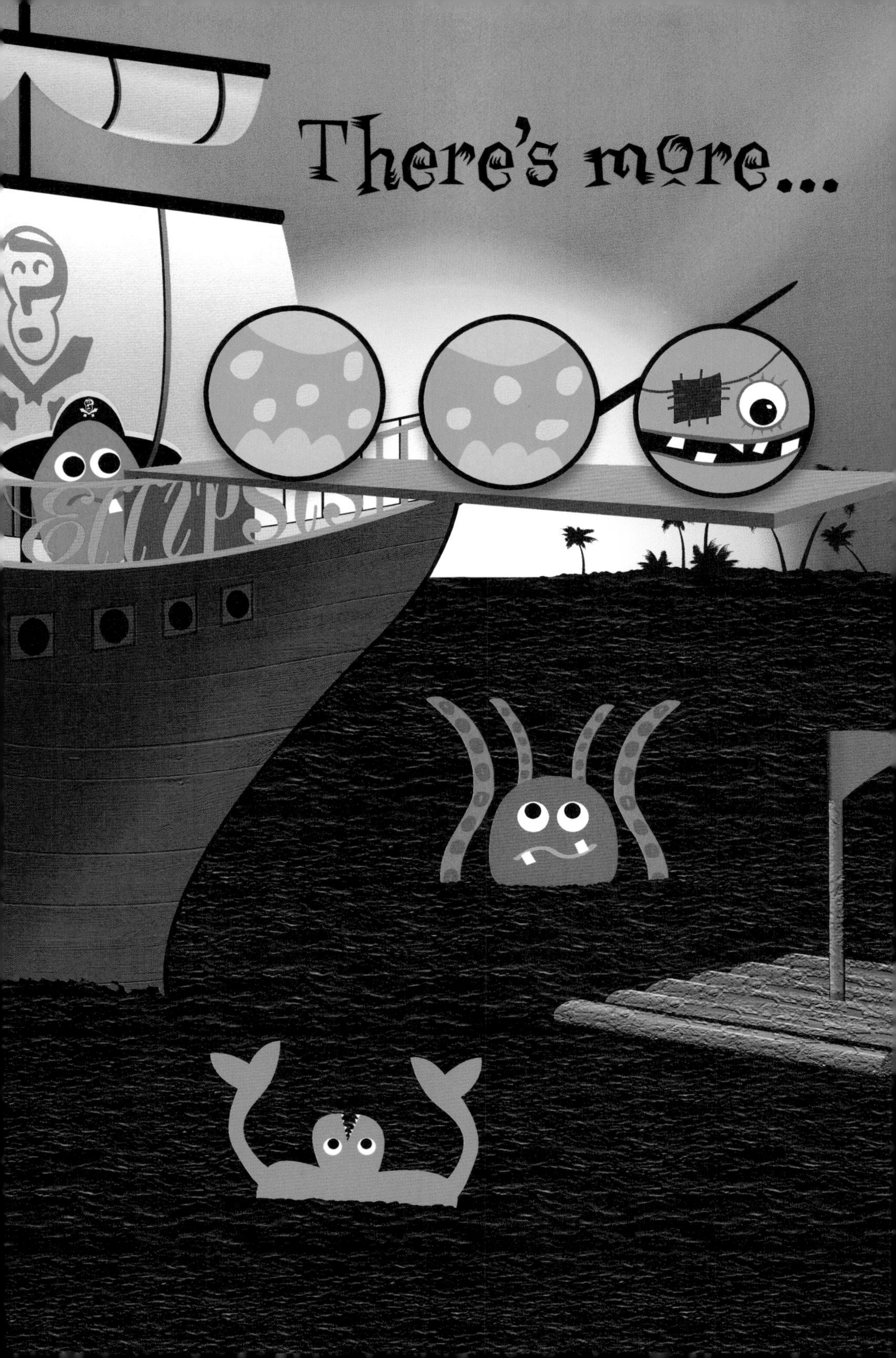
There's more...

Square Brackets

[ ]

Other names: Closed Brackets, Hard Brackets
Crotchet (historical name)

Best Known For: Inserting explanations

Other Uses: Indicating changes to quoted text by the author (often to shorten a quote or to explain the context or language used).

[sic] is used to indicate that a quote has been used precisely including the errors.

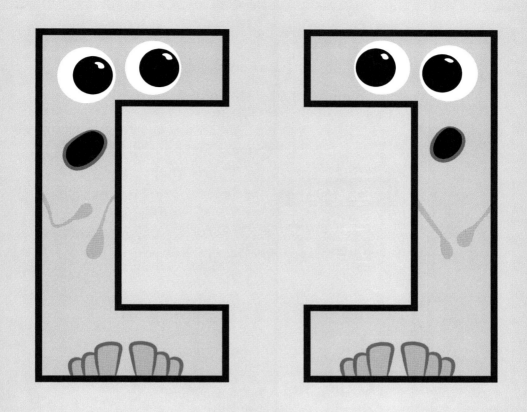

Square Brackets

[ ]

Interesting Stuff:

A variation on curved brackets (see page 44), square brackets enable us to use different types of brackets to distinguish various additions and changes to text.

The term [sic] is taken from the Latin 'sic erat scriptum' meaning 'this it was written'. It indicates that a quote has been used purposefully unchanged (but is also used by people to highlight errors by others [like a pompous snigger]).

For those that prefer to be less obnoxious, square brackets can be used to [discretely] modify mistakes in quoted text. For example "He love[s] it."

There are other shapes of brackets too:

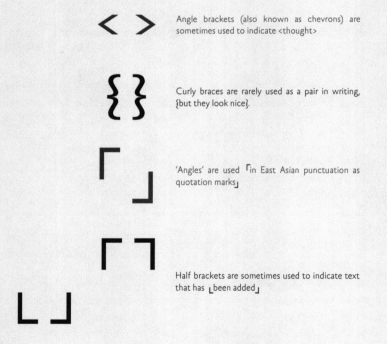

Angle brackets (also known as chevrons) are sometimes used to indicate <thought>

Curly braces are rarely used as a pair in writing, {but they look nice}.

'Angles' are used ⌜in East Asian punctuation as quotation marks⌟

Half brackets are sometimes used to indicate text that has ⌞been added⌟

[AN EXPLANATION]

Slash

/

Other names: Virgule, Forward Slash, Stroke, Oblique, Diagonal

Best Known For: Separating alternatives:

Other Uses: ⟩ Joining names eg. The Johnson/Smith Show

⟩ Dividing dates and fractions

⟩ To indicate a line break when quoting poetry

⟩ As part of an internet web address

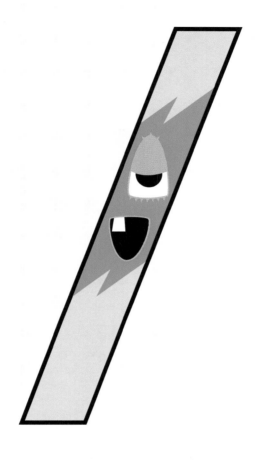

Slash

/

Interesting Stuff:

The slash is the grandparent to the dash and a distant cousin to the comma.

It started life during Roman times and continued to be used into the 19th century as a comma (one slash) / and as a dash // (represented by two slashes).

The double-slashes rotated over time to look like an = before eventually becoming just the one horizontal line and taking shape as the modern single dash –.

Prior to decimalisation in Britain, a slash (known as a 'shilling mark') was used to separate shillings from pence.

The shilling mark is also known as a 'solidus' and is less steep than the forward slash.

The solidus didn't make it on to typewriters and was generally replaced by the forward slash.

As with all punctuation marks the usage of dashes/ slashes varied between writers/printers and developed further over time. After being replaced by the modern comma and dash, the slash has continued to develop and today it is a navigational feature of internet addresses where it indicates the structure or 'pathway' of an address:

www.monsterpunctuation.co.uk/resources/sheet1

Virgule is derived from the Latin 'virga' meaning ' a little stick.

In writing it is often used to represent either/or. This is possibly a legacy of its confused history/ background.

The French comma is called a 'virgule' but uses the same shape as the English comma

Comma/dash/forward slash.
Confused smiley :-/

Separating/alternatives

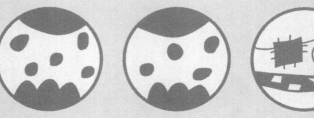

Activity Ideas

Create a New Punctuation Mark

Create a brand new punctuation mark. Think about what the mark will do, how it will be used and what it looks like.

Write a paragraph using your new punctuation mark!

A worksheet can be downloaded for this activity from: www.monsterpunctuation.co.uk

Make Punctuation Stories

Write, draw or perform stories featuring your favourite punctuation monsters. Think about their personalities and the adventures they might have together.

Make Punctuation Patterns

Draw shapes and pictures using only punctuation marks.

Reorganise Sentences

Create a long sentence and print off each word onto a sheet of paper. Print off a copy of each punctuation mark on separate sheets.

Encourage students to rearrange the words and use punctuation marks in different places to experiment with how the meaning and comprehension can be altered.

Create Your Own Punctuation Monster

Students can create their own Punctuation Monsters using these worksheets. Encourage them to think about what different punctuation marks do and the type of personality they might have — for example a full stop might be LOUD or solid like a big rock.

The worksheets can be downloaded for free from:

www.monsterpunctuation.co.uk

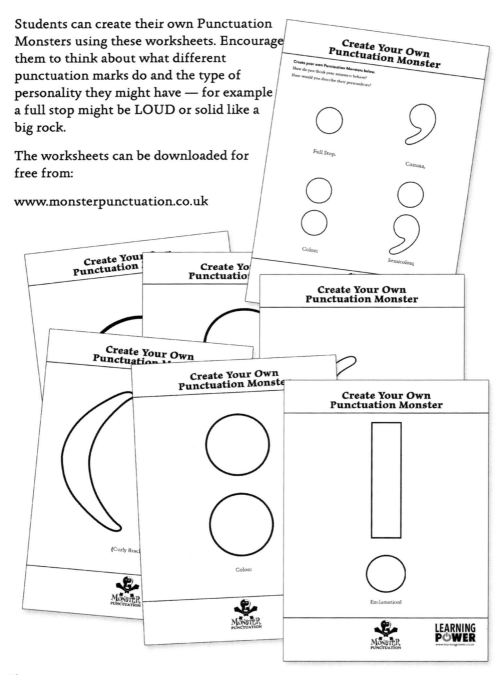

Colouring Sheets

These colouring sheets feature variations in shape of punctuation marks by using different typefaces.

Great for helping students practise the shapes of punctuation marks and for eye catching class displays.

There are 12 different sheets and they can be downloaded for free from:

www.monsterpunctuation.co.uk

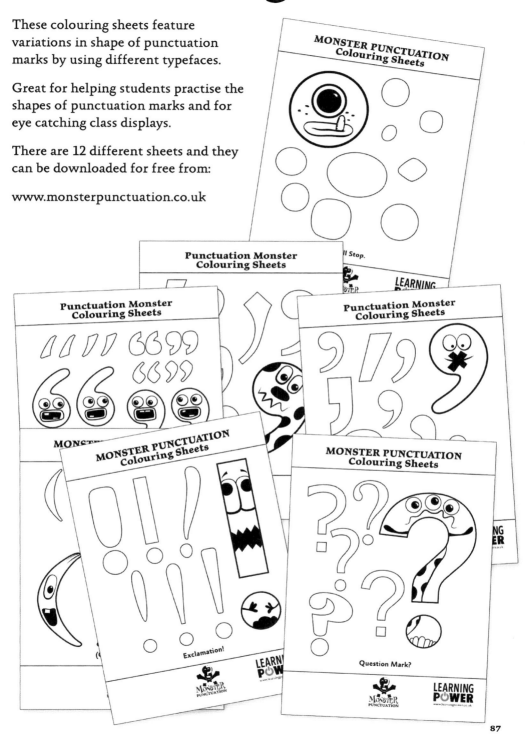

Display Posters

7872002R00050

Printed in Great Britain
by Amazon.co.uk, Ltd.,
Marston Gate.